EXPLORING THE WORLD OF

Elephants

Tracy C. Read

FIREFLY BOOKS

A FIREFLY BOOK

Published by Firefly Books Ltd. 2017
Copyright © 2017 Firefly Books Ltd.
Text copyright © 2017 Tracy C. Read

First printing

Publisher Cataloging-in-Publication Data (U.S.)
Names: Read, Tracy C., author.
Title: Exploring the World of Elephants / Tracy C. Read.
Description: Richmond Hill, Ontario, Canada : Firefly Books, 2017. | Series: Exploring the world of --- | Includes index. | Summary: "Up-close images and fascinating facts about elephants" – Provided by publisher.
Identifiers: ISBN 978-1-77085-944-9 (hardcover) | 978-1-77085-945-6 (paperback)
Subjects: LCSH: Elephants – Juvenile literature.
Classification: LCC QL737.P98R433 | DDC 599.67 – dc23

Library and Archives Canada Cataloguing in Publication
Read, Tracy C., author
    Exploring the world of elephants / Tracy C. Read.
Includes index.
ISBN 978-1-77085-944-9 (hardcover).--ISBN 978-1-77085-945-6 (softcover)
    1. Elephants--Juvenile literature. I. Title.
QL737.P98R42 2017   j599.67   C2017-902460-4

Published in the United States by
Firefly Books (U.S.) Inc.
P.O. Box 1338, Ellicott Station, Buffalo, New York 14205

Published in Canada by
Firefly Books Ltd.
50 Staples Avenue, Unit 1, Richmond Hill, Ontario L4B 0A7

Cover and interior design: Janice McLean/Bookmakers Press Inc.

Printed in China

Canada We acknowledge the financial support of the Government of Canada.

For Kate, who knows that a mother's love makes the world go round.

CONTENTS

INTRODUCTION: EARTH'S LARGEST LAND ANIMALS
MEET THE ELEPHANTS 4

WHAT MAKES AN ELEPHANT AN ELEPHANT?
ANATOMY LESSON 6

HOW ELEPHANTS MAKE THE MOST OF THEIR SENSES
NATURAL TALENTS 10

MATING AND FAMILY LIFE
MOTHER KNOWS BEST 14

DIET AND DISTRIBUTION
EATING MACHINES 18

ELEPHANTS AT RISK
IN DEFENSE OF GIANTS 22

INDEX AND PHOTO CREDITS 24

SAFE HAVEN
This herd of African bush elephants has room to wander in southwestern Kenya's Maasai Mara, a wildlife sanctuary bordered by Serengeti National Park to the south.

MEET THE ELEPHANTS

Powerful, intelligent, resourceful and social, elephants have captivated humans for thousands of years. We've featured them in ancient and modern artworks and used them as symbols in our religions and myths. In some cultures, we've put them to work as beasts of burden; in others, we've made them beasts of war.

Perhaps some of our fascination is based on the fact that elephants and humans have a great deal in common. We both live long lives and cherish our nuclear and extended families. Our offspring benefit from a long childhood, during which they are taught life skills that are personal and practical. We both dwell in communities, and we enjoy a wide range of foods and habitats. We share the risk of heart disease and arthritis, and we have the capacity to mourn our dead.

The elephant's ancestors once lived on every continent but Antarctica and Australia. A few centuries ago, millions of elephants ranged from the shores of the Mediterranean all the way through Africa to the Cape of Good Hope. Today, two genuses endure: the African elephant and the Asian elephant. Roughly 400,000 African forest and African bush elephants live in a patchwork of national parks in Africa, while some 40,000 Asian elephants struggle to survive in Southeast Asia.

Let's find out why the battle to save the majestic elephant is one worth waging.

FAMILY MEETING AT THE WATERING HOLE

Finding a water source is at the top of the to-do list for the herd's matriarch. An adult elephant can drink nine quarts (8.5 L) of water with each trunkful, while a calf is able to draw in three quarts (2.8 L). These African elephants may have been summoned from afar with a low, rumbling call from their leader.

ANATOMY LESSON

With its massive head and torso, huge ears, long trunk and tail and sturdy legs and feet, the largest land animal on Earth is also one of the planet's most unusual-looking creatures.

Perhaps the elephant's most notable feature is its trunk. This bone-free appendage is a combined upper lip and snout. Made up of more than 100,000 muscle bundles, it is powerful enough to pull a tree from its roots. The tip of the African elephant's trunk has two fingerlike projections (the Asian elephant has one), the better to pick up food. The elephant uses its trunk to smell, breathe and deliver food and liquids to its mouth. The trunk is also an impressive noisemaker, trumpeting ear-shattering sounds for miles. A powerful swimmer, the elephant uses its trunk as a snorkel as it crosses rivers.

An elephant's teeth include its two lengthy incisors, known as tusks, useful for digging, foraging for food and frightening off its few enemies. Over the course of its long life, an elephant has six different sets of molars that gradually wear down and are replaced.

Sturdy and sure-footed on all terrains, from swamps and deserts to forests and mountainsides, an elephant in a hurry resorts to a blend of walking and running. Although it never has all four feet off the ground at the same time, an African bull can reach speeds of 30 miles per hour (48 km/h).

HEAD TO TOE

The skin of an Asian elephant, above, loses pigmentation as the animal ages, leaving pink freckles around its eyes and trunk. Below: The huge, spongy pad of an elephant's foot expands on contact to help distribute its great weight.

NATURE'S SUNSCREEN

To defend their sensitive skin from the hot sun and annoying insects, elephants use their trunks to blow dust over themselves as a protective coating. For a cooling shower, they draw up large volumes of water and spray it over their backs.

Brain
The elephant's well-developed brain is the largest brain of any land mammal. Known for its intelligence, long-term memory and ability to use tools, the elephant is also highly social.

Ears
An elephant stays cool by flapping its ears to fan its body and lower its blood temperature. The African elephant's much larger ears sit higher on its head than do the Asian elephant's.

Height
An African elephant can reach 13 feet (4 m) at the shoulder; an Asian elephant reaches 11½ feet (3.5 m).

Heart
An elephant's heart beats at a rate of about 30 beats per minute.

Weight
An adult African male elephant weighs from 8,820 to 15,430 pounds (4,000–7,000 kg), while the Asian adult male weighs from 6,615 to 11,020 pounds (3,000–5,000 kg).

Tusks
An African male, or bull, elephant's tusk can be 11½ feet (3.5 m) long and weigh 220 pounds (100 kg). The African female's tusks are smaller, as are the male Asian's.

Trunk
An up to 7-foot-long (2 m) snout that can weigh 400 pounds (181 kg), an elephant's trunk is a mass of more than 100,000 muscle bundles.

The African elephant, facing page, and the Asian elephant, below, are distinct in several ways. While the African elephant's head is smooth and rounded and its back is concave, the Asian's head is crumpled and its back is flat or convex. The African elephant's skin is deeply wrinkled compared with the much smoother skin of the Asian elephant.

Skin
As thick as an inch (2.5 cm) in some places and paper thin in others, an elephant's skin is extremely sensitive.

Tail
Tipped with coarse hair, the elephant's long tail is a built-in flyswatter.

Digestive system
The elephant's stomach is a holding tank for the hundreds of pounds of food it eats each day. Its intestines are roughly 100 feet (30.5 m) long.

Teeth
Over a lifetime, an adult elephant's brick-sized teeth are replaced five times, with molars sliding forward to replace older, worn-down teeth.

Feet
The elephant is remarkably sure-footed on all terrains. Its front legs bend at the "wrist," and it can deliver sharp, hard kicks with its front feet.

NATURAL TALENTS

How does the largest land animal on Earth use its five senses to gather information?

Given the physical real estate taken up by the elephant's trunk, it shouldn't surprise us that smell is one of this animal's most developed senses. Researchers have found that the elephant has twice as many genes dedicated to picking up a scent as man's best friend, the super-sniffing dog. By waving its trunk in the air and breathing deeply, an elephant can zero in on a water source that is miles away.

It also uses its sense of smell to find food, to identify family members and to detect predators or enemies. An elephant's startle response may well be its reaction to a scent it recognizes as unfriendly.

Scent plays a part in courtship and mating as well. All elephants have a scent gland behind each eye, and periodically, the male releases an oily secretion through these glands that signals an aggressive eagerness to find a mate. The female also sends out scent signals to indicate her readiness to start a family.

Its oversized ears are a sign that hearing is likewise important to the elephant, whose lifestyle involves nonstop travel in search of food and water, often separated from its extended family. Staying in touch is critical. An elephant's hearing is geared to low frequencies called infrasonic sounds. In what is sometimes referred to as its "secret language," an elephant

TRUNK BUMPS
For an elephant family, touch is an important part of everyday life. By entwining their trunks, these two young calves are learning a lot about each other. At the same time, they're pleasantly establishing what may well be a lifelong bond.

can hear—and generate—messages that can be heard from a great distance. With its soft and loud rumbles, long and urgent contact calls, pulsating signals and short and sharp trumpeting, an elephant has a large vocabulary.

Highly sensitive skin covers the elephant's body, and this extremely social animal doesn't hold back from public displays of affection when in the company of friends and relatives. A gathering of elephants can be a love-in, with rubbing and the gentle and enthusiastic exchange of trunk touches.

With average eyesight, the elephant prefers the muted light of dawn and late afternoon to the bright sun. Even so, an elephant is skilled at recognizing a wide range of visual signals sent by other elephants through slight adjustments in the head, eyes, mouth, ears, tusks, trunk, tail and feet.

Not much is known about an elephant's sense of taste, but the taste buds on its tongue suggest that the elephant is not indifferent to the quality of its food.

ALL EARS
Above: Called to a water hole by the matriarch, a group of elephants, above, drinks deep when it has the chance. Right: This bull elephant is a man on a mission—it's mating season. With ears on the alert, he is better able to funnel surrounding sounds.

SMELL
With its long proboscis, the elephant may have the keenest sense of smell of all mammals.

TOUCH
The surface of an elephant's skin is rich with nerve endings, and this animal enjoys lots of contact with its family members.

SIGHT
Average, at best. It doesn't help that an elephant's large ears may interfere when it turns to see what's behind it.

TASTE
An elephant's tongue has taste buds, and some elephants show a preference for specific foods, suggesting they know what they like.

HEARING
An elephant hears sounds humans can't and communicates with low rumbles that can be detected from afar by other elephants.

MOTHER KNOWS BEST

Across a windswept African savanna, a mature, robust male elephant raises his trunk to the sky and sniffs. Nearby, a female elephant has entered a cycle called estrus, and her body is releasing chemicals that advertise she is ready to reproduce. Lust is in the air, and the male is soon on the move.

Twice as large as the female, the male African elephant continues to grow his whole life, which may be up to 60 years. Proving his physical superiority is part of the courtship ritual and a chance for him to pass along his genes to the next generation.

Arriving at the female's side, he aggressively faces down any younger male competitors. It's a display he repeats for the benefit of many females throughout the year.

Mate selection is a far more significant decision for the female. Depending on the local climate and food resources, estrus occurs only three or four times a year and lasts less than a week. The female invests roughly 22 months preparing to give birth and several more years nurturing her calf and readying it for life, so it's vital that she chooses the fittest specimen to father her young.

Courtship may last a few hours or a day, but the act of mating itself is over quickly. The male then returns to his solitary life and has no part in raising his offspring.

The female, meanwhile, remains with her herd of some 10 elephants, giving birth almost two

PLAYS WELL WITH OTHERS

A young African elephant, top, indulges in some gentle rough-housing with one of its cousins, while an older Asian elephant calf, above, mirrors its mother's behavior at a stream. An elephant's childhood is all about learning through doing.

TRUNK TRAINING

Weighing about 250 pounds (110 kg) when it is born, an elephant calf has poor vision and is briefly a little unsteady on its feet. One of the newborn's first jobs is to find its mother's nipples through scent and touch, and for that, it needs to stand. Next, it has to learn how to flop its trunk onto its forehead so that it doesn't interfere with suckling, which it does with its mouth. Learning how to make its highly complex trunk do everything it is capable of doing takes a calf six to eight months of endless experimentation.

LOVE ME TENDER
Wrapping its trunk around its mother's, this Asian elephant calf reinforces their bond. Until the age of three months, a calf is completely dependent on its mother for nutrition. Then it starts to experiment by tasting vegetation and may use its trunk to take food from its mother's mouth and carry it to its own. A calf may nurse for three to four years, and some return for comfort suckling for several more.

years later, usually to a single calf. Elephants organize their family lives around females, typically led by the oldest female, the matriarch. She is revered for her long memory and her sound decision-making skills, honed over many years of keeping her family fed and watered and together.

Female calves stay with their mothers for their entire lives, but males are driven out of the herd when they reach puberty. At that point, they live on their own or join up with several other teenaged males until adulthood.

When a new calf arrives, the family may assist with the birth, welcoming the newborn with affectionate touches and excited trumpeting. The aunts, older sisters, cousins and grandmother are very much involved in making sure this new life flourishes.

A calf depends on its mother's milk until it is about the age of two, when vegetation has become a regular part of its diet. A growing calf gleefully explores its surroundings, and daily life includes vigorous play wrestling and tumbling bouts with other calves as well as life lessons in swimming, bathing and wielding its trunk to deliver water to its mouth.

When a herd grows too big, it may split into two, but these extended families often travel close together, communicating through rumblings and calls. A family reunion, even if only after a few hours' separation, is a time for great excitement and joy, just as a family death is a time of deep sorrow and grief.

FAMILY RULES

Whether on the move or settling in for the night, adult elephants keep their young in the center of the herd, safe from harm. Touching is an important form of communication, and adults regularly touch, stroke and pat their young. Occasionally, a gentle kick or trunk slap is used to discipline a youngster that misbehaves.

EATING MACHINES

The world's largest land animal does not tread lightly on the planet, but why would it? A keystone species, the elephant has a crucial impact on the lives of all the other organisms that share its ecosystem, from plants and animals to humans.

This megaherbivore grazes and browses its way across the landscape in search of the hundreds of pounds of food it needs for fuel each day. Grinding up grasses, brush, bark, tree branches, fruit and seedlings with its massive molars, it can't help transforming every neighborhood through which it passes.

On the vast, open landscape of the African savanna, the elephant feeds on sprouting trees and shrubs, digging up roots with its tusks and doing its part to maintain a healthy grassland that is home to countless other wildlife species.

In its ever-shrinking forest habitat, the smaller African forest elephant browses on the canopy, opening natural gaps in the dense vegetation, letting in the sunlight and creating opportunities for new growth.

In the dry season, an elephant resorts to the tools at hand. With its preferred tusk (an elephant typically favors one or the other, just as we prefer using our left or right hand), it digs for water, leaving behind a pool that other animals struggling to survive a drought can also enjoy.

In the scrublands, rainforests

PASS THE SALT
To augment its need for sodium and other minerals, an Asian elephant, top, nibbles at the soil in a salt marsh, a common behavior in all elephants. Two young calves, above, tag along as an adult African elephant grazes contentedly.

HUNGRY HERBIVORE

An elephant forages along the Chobe River in Botswana's Chobe National Park, home to one of Africa's largest, most diverse concentrations of game. According to the 2016 Great Elephant Census, the elephant population in Botswana remains stable.

CHEW TIME
A trio of elephants, above left, feeds on the wet season's high-protein grass in Serengeti National Park, Tanzania. Above right: A male exploits both his ability to stand on his hind legs and his telescoping trunk to browse up to 20 feet (6 m) off the ground.

and grasslands of Southeast Asia, the small population of surviving wild Asian elephants performs the same functions.

With its huge metabolism, the elephant is an eating machine. Not surprisingly, it is also a defecating marvel, leaving roughly 22 pounds (10 kg) of waste in its wake some 15 to 20 times a day. Its digestive system is not particularly efficient, which means that many seeds pass through untouched, making the elephant one of nature's great natural propagators.

There's a downside, of course. If the elephant is unable to find the sustenance it needs, it is more than willing to feed on anything in its path, uprooting cultivated

An overheated African elephant takes advantage of a water hole in South Africa's Kruger National Park, one of the largest game reserves on the continent, to bathe and drink deep. Depending on the temperature, an adult African elephant may take in between 20 and 60 gallons (75–225 L) of water a day. An Asian elephant may consume up to 80 gallons (300 L) a day.

tree plantings and gobbling up farmers' crops. As we humans, in turn, convert the elephant's natural habitat to our own purposes, it's easy to see the complex conflicts that can develop.

What is the solution? In Africa, a growing appreciation for the economic benefits of conservation offers some hope. Roughly 70 percent of Africa's elephants live in southern Africa, with an estimated 225,000 living in what has been described as "one of the most ambitious ecological experiments on the planet"—the Kavango-Zambezi Transfrontier Conservation Area. A shared project among Angola, Botswana, Namibia, Zambia and Zimbabwe, its goal is to stitch together corridors that will allow elephant populations to peaceably travel between protected areas. Ideally, this will result in a reduction in the stress humans and elephants cause one another as they compete for the same territory. And ecotourism visitors to Africa will experience elephants in their natural habitat.

IN DEFENSE OF GIANTS

The current perilous state of the elephant is a complex story, and humans are at the center of it.

African elephants once lived in peace with humans, sharing the rich resources of the vast continent of Africa. That relationship began to shift in the 18th and early 19th centuries, when European traders and colonialists arrived to exploit African people as well as the land and its wildlife. When the ivory from the elephants' tusks was arbitrarily deemed a luxury item, the lives of these majestic creatures changed forever. Hundreds of thousands of slaughtered elephants have paid the price.

Despite efforts by conservationists to halt the ivory trade, an African elephant population estimated at 1.3 million in 1979 has fallen to some 400,000 today. An international ban on the trade in 1989 has been widely violated by poachers wielding automatic rifles to capitalize on vulnerable wildlife and the human appetite for ivory trinkets. Thankfully, China's decision to stop its trade in ivory by the end of 2017 represents a major victory.

But there are other factors that may be even harder to fix. Political upheaval in African countries, habitat fragmentation resulting from human activities, such as farming and mining, and the impact of climate change are all critical pieces of the conservation challenge. A massive migratory animal needs room to roam, and less than 20 percent of the African elephant's former habitat is now protected.

Similarly, widespread deforestation across Southeast Asia has left wild Asian elephants few places to live. Some elephants still have a role in cultural celebrations, but many captive elephants are put on display in circuses, orphanages and sanctuaries. And private citizens who own elephants struggle to feed and house them in an economy where the demand for elephant labor is in a steep decline.

UP IN SMOKE

In April 2016, the Government of Kenya ordered the burning of ivory from about 8,000 elephants killed by poachers. Even if the ivory trade is successfully eliminated, African elephants still face a multitude of challenges, from fragmented habitat and drought to conflict with human communities.

LAID OFF

Once gainfully employed in the logging industry, many Asian elephants, like the one shown in chains, above, have been thrown out of work as a result of deforestation. Left: Asian elephants enjoy a moment of unshackled freedom as they bathe at an orphanage where the public pays a fee to view them.

affection, displays of, 10, 12, 16, 17
Africa, 4, 21, 22
African bush elephant, 3, 4
African elephant, 4, 5, 8, 9, 14, 18, 21, 22, 23
   population of, 22
African forest elephant, 4, 18
anatomy, 6
ancestors, 4
Angola, 21
Asian elephant, 4, 6, 8, 9, 14, 16, 18, 20, 21, 22, 23
Botswana, 19, 21
brain, 8
calves, 5, 10, 14, 15, 16, 17, 18
Cape of Good Hope, 4
China, 22
Chobe National Park, 19
communication, 5, 12, 13, 17
   visual signals, 12
conservation of, 22
courtship behaviors, 10, 14
diet, 16, 17, 18, 20, 21
digestive system, 9, 20
ears, 8, 10, 12
estrus, 14
excrement, 20

exploitation of, 22
family life, 16, 17
feet, 6, 9
gestation period, 14
Great Elephant Census (2016), 19
growth of, 14
habitat
   impact on, 18, 20
   reduction of, 22, 23
hearing, sense of, 10, 13
heart, 8
height, 8
herd size, 14, 17
humans and elephants, 4, 21, 22, 23
intestines, length of, 9
ivory trade, 22, 23
Kavango-Zambezi Transfrontier Conservation Area, 21
Kenya, 3, 23
Kruger National Park, 21
locomotion, 6
   speed, 6
logging industry, use in, 22, 23
longevity, 14
Maasai Mara, 3
matriarch, 5, 12, 16

Mediterranean, 4
Namibia, 21
Serengeti National Park, 3, 20
scent gland, 10
sight, sense of, 12, 13, 15
skin, 6, 7, 9, 12, 13
smell, sense of, 10, 13, 15
South Africa, 21
Southeast Asia, 4, 20, 22
tail, 9
Tanzania, 20
taste, sense of, 12, 13
teeth, 6, 9, 18
touch, sense of, 10, 13, 15
trunk, 6, 7, 8, 10, 15, 16, 20
   capacity of (liquid), 5
tusks, 6, 8, 18, 22
vocalizations.
   See communication
water consumption, 21
weight, 8, 15
Zambia, 21
Zimbabwe, 21